BRADFORD & BEYOND

For Cathy

Also by Gerard Benson

Name Game (1971)

Gorgon (1984)

This Poem Doesn't Rhyme (Editor, 1990)

Poems on the Underground
(Joint Editor, six editions, 1991, 1992, 1993, 1994, 1995, 1996)

The Magnificent Callisto (1992)

Does W Trouble You? (Editor, 1994)

Evidence of Elephants (1995)

In Wordsworth's Chair (1995, reprinted 1996)

Love Poems on the Underground (Joint Editor, 1996)

London Poems on the Underground (Joint Editor, 1996)

Comic Poems on the Underground (Joint Editor, 1996)

Nemo's Almanac 1997 (Editor, 1996)

Nemo's Almanac 1998 (Editor, 1997)

BRADFORD & BEYOND

A Sonnet Journal

Gerard Benson

FLAMBARD

ACKNOWLEDGEMENTS

Some of these poems have appeared in the following publications:
The Friend, New Statesman, Pivot, Poetry Wales.

Sonnet 65 was a prize winner in the Scottish National
Open Poetry Competition, 1996.

Gerard Benson would like to express his gratitude to Sally Baker
of the Taliesin Trust at Tŷ Newydd for her help and support.
Grateful thanks are also due to the Authors' Foundation whose grant
was of considerable financial help, enabling the writer to have time
to concentrate without distraction during the revision.

Flambard Press wishes to thank Northern Arts for its financial support.

Published in Great Britain in 1997 by Flambard Press
4 Mitchell Avenue, Jesmond, Newcastle upon Tyne NE2 3LA

Typeset by Barbara Sumner
Cover design by Catherine Benson
Cover processed by Mike Davis

Printed in Great Britain by Cromwell Press, Broughton Gifford,
Melksham, Wiltshire

A CIP catalogue record for this book is available from the British Library

ISBN 1 873226 26 8

© Gerard Benson 1997

◆ 1 ◆

Tonight a helicopter, red and green lights
winking and flashing, patrols the allotments.
Police. Flying very low. For several nights
they have played this game. This is a dodgy catchment;
the yards and back lanes make a tortuous warren.
Probably gangs of kids, small thieves. Or users.
Or are fresh riots brewing (a terror common
round here)? But it's most likely drug abusers.
Or dealers. Or the fuzz, having a little fun,
playing searchlights and walky-talkies,
growling in the sky, putting the frighteners on
the dealers and teenage gangs. Mullarkey.
Impressive, though. You hear the roar repeat,
echoing back from terraced Naples Street.

◆ 2 ◆

There are rows of terraced houses in the area,
back-to-backs, a labyrinth of alleys
and broken fences. Kids playing out. Big families.
There's petty crime but the cops are scarier,
crouched above us in their raucous helicopter,
circling, wheeling like playground bullies,
drenching dry gardens in light, creating malaise.
But perhaps it's not kids they are after.
Is there an armed prowler on the street,
a killer on the loose? Imagination escalates.
We hurry indoors, turn keys in locks. Quite suddenly
the chopper moves off, southward across the city;
a cop car, hidden till now, accelerates
along Ashwell Road, following. Mission complete.

The garden is bright with dew. There's Bach on the radio
(a Brandenberg); the postman's lenient;
better, he brings a hefty cheque: convenient,
and only just in time; bills to be paid-i-oh,
tra-la. Autumn's offering a few discounted
leaves and a breeze, no more; the sun's brilliant.
With my back to all this gold I sort through millions
of sheets of paper, well maybe a thousand –
bills, letters, articles, drafts of poems, clutter
of cuttings, doodles; higgledy-piggledy, any-old-how.
Quite unable to make any real decisions
I shuffle the papers from one pile to another,
return a contract, turn off the radio (Lutyens now
instead of Bach). Return to my tunnel vision.

A day on the treadmill: but, infinitely distractible,
I diversify a little – change a bulb, mend
a trowel, dig up couch grass, buy bin bags, send
off poems with s.a.e.s, trying to redouble
and reinforce my bulwarks against idleness
(that first infirmity of troubled minds),
too aware that beyond this room all kinds
of disastrous things are happening – distress
on a scale that I'm not equipped to think about,
in remote locations; Sarajevo, where Nato
is currently hurling lethal weapons at Serbians
who have themselves murdered their fellow Yugoslavians;
Muraroa, where Chirac demonstrates his nuclear clout.
But, I ask you, what the hell can *I* do?

◆ 5 ◆

In Marshal Tito Street, says today's *Independent*,
Maja Desancic, aged eight, can peep between the sandbags
in the facade of the newly opened Benetton's.
(But Sarajevan shoppers need cash in their handbags:
'No credit cards. This is war,' an assistant said.)
Little Maja is a lovely child; her face
is sweet, mischievous. I hope she won't be dead
by the time this poem is written. It's a race
against the clock for us all, but for some the odds
are shorter. What else is in the paper?
More Labour leaks, the sour revenge of an Aids
victim, *la bombe française*. But it's that pert picture
of Maja, her eyes alight with curiosity,
her chances so bleak, that's printed in the memory.

◆ 6 ◆

On the train to London the four-seater table
opposite ours is rowdily occupied by clergy
who have been attending a conference. Their decibel
count is superb, whether debating Christ and Sociology,
the Freud/Jung schism as it affects Christians,
or merely joshing and barking with laughter;
for noise pollution they trounce football fans,
and give a close run to poser-phone orators.
Did you know old notions of transubstantiation
had been, in a sense, transcended? It was news to me.
You could have knocked me down with a crozier.
At Kings Cross things don't look any rosier.
A beggar at the ticket machine in the tube station
squats like a toll man, extracting a conscience fee.

◆ 7 ◆

An *incident* has halted all trains in either
direction on the Victoria Line. So we find
another route, struggling in something of a dither,
with heavy cases through herds of resigned
travellers. They call us customers. The name defines
our function. And what signifies this word 'incident'?
Suicide attempt? Fire? Flooding on the lines?
Driver collapsed at the controls? Management
taken over by Martians? Or multinationals? Be sure
of this: tomorrow's papers will not enlighten us.
It is too common. Not news any more.
(And water on the rails might frighten us;
it's a potent mixture, water and electricity.)
Come back, you clerical customers, and pray for the city.

◆ 8 ◆

Chess with my host. Merely a game but my
adrenaline races like mad; my heart
pounds as I punch the clock; my mouth goes dry.
A ritual drama's being acted out.
I hesitate to cite *The Golden Bough*
but more is happening than two old friends
at play. An atavistic deed somehow
sneaks in, between our gambits and our ends.
Checkmate! Shah Mat! The king is dead! Long live
the king! We hold a quick post-mortem, then
we put the pieces up and play again,
bargain our pawns, then spar and try to spring
cunning surprises; fiercely combative,
we enact once more the murder of a king.

And while we play, late on a Friday night,
we hear the sirens of the fire brigade,
and ambulances shrieking up the road,
and raucous street gangs angling for a fight,
who pass us by, thank God. Huw takes my knight.
Recapturing will fracture my blockade.
I shove the pieces back and turn the board,
no point in playing on. My turn for white.
And on the train, travelling back to Bradford,
I scan the papers. Though short on policies,
the Education Secretary's active;
she has a plan, suggests her colleagues use
(I quote verbatim) 'words people find attractive'
and offers: *standards, discipline,* and *choice.*

◆ 10 ◆

We're hurrying north. The sky is dark, and full
of long, flat-bottomed clouds, some very low,
gravid with rain. They rear, fantastical,
a snorting dragon, giant fist, banjo,
disintegrating face. They twist and bend,
the whole odd metamorphic show
replete with inexplicable portent,
a gnomic message from above, or so
it seems. Difficult not to read some meaning
into a pageant of such vividness
(a cockerel's head becomes a pig's behind).
So what? The relevance is in the mind,
not in the outside world (weather or chess).
Now we've passed Wakefield and it's really raining.

◆ 11 ◆

'Attractive words: discipline, standards, choice.'
It's a free country and the range is wide.
You choose your heap and I'll choose a Rolls-Royce.
And as to discipline, friend, I'll decide
how it will be achieved. I'll make the rules.
That is my job, while yours is to obey.
I mean to raise the standards in our schools,
which have deteriorated since my day;
but I shan't tackle problems in society
which might have caused the problems: not my job.
Opt out and I will offer you variety:
discipline, standards, choice. Och, whisht your gob.
On the receiving end these dull reactive
reflex proposals feel far less attractive.

◆ 12 ◆

The last night of the Proms: a sludgy mix
of sentiment and music, poignant, though.
Blake's fervour (devilish mills and burning bow)
serves for a jingoistic singalong. It sticks
in my craw. And yet these patriotic tricks,
Rule Britannia, Elgar's march, *maestoso*,
just work; I melt, *molto affettuoso*.
I douse the radio but I've had my fix.
That was on Saturday. Sunday brings
its own events. A hopeful medical
centre in Manningham that's combating
addiction holds an Open Day. We call,
offer ideas. And, in the evening,
Joan Armatrading at St George's Hall.

Joan Armatrading at St George's Hall,
and we are in front stalls with the fans
(having sneaked downstairs in the interval).
Joan takes the mike in eloquent dark hands,
begins her first song, cool, restrained. Guitars,
percussion, keyboards ride along with her.
The songs change: some are sweet, some quirky. There's
that swift staccato burst, that soaring slur
that lifts a high note on an endless breath;
then schmaltzy strings, then energy again.
You've had a mournful year. Your father's death
was hard. Your grief was laced with physical pain.
And there were other anguishes. But now,
just now, we live these songs, my arm round you.

My arm round you because I want it so,
because I love you, and because the music,
which knows all that a human needs to know,
tells me I should; the sound and not the lyric
guides my action. All the world is rhythmic.
A cellist throbs. A fiddler plies her bow.
Joan sings. The hall's charged with emotive static.
Music hath charms. I put my arm round you.
The tenuous spell is broken by applause
and whistling and whooping, and the beat
alters again, fierce now. And there are wars
outside this hall, and anger on the street,
and there is very little I can do.
Because I can, I put my arm round you.

◆ 15 ◆

Down Naples Street this morning to buy
the daily paper (wondering, will our water
be cut off? they've applied for a drought order),
I feel a tang in the air. I can't say why,
but the very socks and pants hung out to dry
say Autumn – something in the way they flutter.
Something in the faces of the people, in their posture
agrees. Summer is over, albeit the sky
is blue today and cloudless, the rowan berries
are bright as new blood. Buses are fuller.
The trees are green. But don't they show the merest
suggestion, no more than that, of yellow,
as if they filtered sunlight? It's autumn but there is
no mist, no fruitfulness. It's not mellow.

◆ 16 ◆

In the evening there's that pinch in the chest.
We're at the equinox; the Summer Triangle
has moved aside. Though in this electric jungle
there are no stars to be seen; it's a processed
sky, which the banks of city lights have messed
into a yellowish glow, not star-spangled,
a muzzy smear. The hemisphere is angled
away from the sun and we're set for that longest
of journeys, outward into the dark and cold.
Bradford, far inland, in sight of the Pennines,
lies at the bottom of a hilly bowl,
rises into its suburbs, often sits dark below
when all the surrounding tops are covered with snow.
But now the season announces itself by various signs,

◆ 17 ◆

by political party conferences; by back-to-school
displays in stationers' windows: brand new protractors
and compasses, shining pencil sets, ruler, slide rule,
school bags, fancy notebooks; and the little actors
in this tragicomedy portrayed with faces as shiny
as the merchandise, with smiles, and socks pulled up,
with badges on their pockets – and nowhere even a tiny
hint that all this aspiration might come unstuck,
like the spines of the paperback dictionaries.
And there are sports kits, shorts and skirts,
and sensational studded shoes, and patterned jerseys
endorsed by millionaire athletes. And it hurts.
But it could come right. And no one should take away
from the complex anticipation of that first day.

◆ 18 ◆

One stanza finishes. Another starts.
They're seamless on the page but the events
may fall behind. My journal is in parts.
Although I'm writing in the present tense,
time intervenes. I scribble in trains, on buses.
I write of Bradford's weather in Grasmere.
(I wrote?) And these Victorian lakeside houses
where I work now, beside an unlit fire,
could figure later. I am trying to tell
some kind of truth, trying to record (for whom?)
these paradoxical times. I write pell-mell
but the result is still too uniform,
too fluent even. Everything's made too pleasant
by this damn tense, this ever-present present.

♦ 19 ♦

'Time present and time past …' et cetera
(apologies to Eliot and Byron),
are both held in this hurrying tense. The future
is not my subject. But how do I environ
everything in the now? And, more than that:
what to leave out? What to include? The bloke
on the bus who argues with himself? My cat?
The football scores? The ozone layer? Coke?
If so, what kind? This brief account of one
short period of my life, this mobile 'now',
is all the time adjusted. It must come
under the censor's hand, which won't allow
some kinds of statement. The pages are full of erasures,
the overall scheme marked by frequent evasions.

♦ 20 ♦

In Grasmere Vale the coalman's busy again;
people are lighting fires; the big grimed lorry
is parked outside Dove Cottage. There is rain
as ever, soft drizzle. A quick flurry
of wind brings a few damp leaves down the lane
from How Top Farm. This autumn will be early
after the droughty summer. Drunks on the train
abruptly change the mood. I shall surely
return to Cumbria's autumn, but right now
(writing this journal on a train to Crewe)
two threatening bruisers terrorise us all.
'Fuck off, you cunt. We've paid our fucking fares!'
they tell the guard. We glance away; we're scared.
'I'll fucking bang you in the fucking balls.'

◆ 21 ◆

Return, Crewe Junction, that dread voice is past.
They staggered off at Wigan, hurled abuse,
a scary duo, but they had their use;
the present tense is justified at last.
I set their phrases down as they were uttered,
hot from those fuming brains; their tongues were thick.
True poets both, they spoke in just pentameters
(juster than most of mine): a curious trick
of the mind. A colleague once defined blank verse:
'the language of the British under stress'
(not merely an imposed device) 'for poetry
draws on obscure and deep linguistic sources.'
And these two fellows with their rhythmic curses
appear to vindicate my colleague's theory.

◆ 22 ◆

Autumn in Grasmere last year was a riot
of vivid colour. All the forest side
blazed in spectacular glory. It's quiet
this year. No reds and oranges collide
in fiery conflict. Rather, green on green
begins to fade. You see the faintest stipple
of umber or of burnt sienna, sheen
of ochreish gold, among the leaves, which ripple
in late September's rising winds. And those
July foxgloves, still vertical, display
a few surprising flowers. A late rose
hangs on the dying hedge for one last day;
and White Moss Common's tinted with seed heads
of the bog asphodel, a rusty red.

◆ 23 ◆

I lag behind myself again, and write
this record of the north in Gwynedd; I'm here
to work with students. I've put an old wheel from a bike
on the oak table. It's cobwebbed, rusty; it lacks a tyre.
The students fondle it, roll it on its rim,
they smell it, or play music on its spokes;
some swiftly glance then pass it on, too prim
to touch a thing so soiled; there are words, jokes,
a gasp when a woodlouse drops onto the table.
We settle and explore; this is a writing course.
The obsolete wheel someone once used is able
to call forth ideas and feelings, metaphors
and riddles, questions about life and time.
One mundane object conjures the sublime.

◆ 24 ◆

I struggle through to consciousness. I'm quite
shockingly awake in my Tŷ Newydd
bedroom, released from ghastly realms of myth
too troubling to suppress. It's been a night
of travel in an unknown, hostile world.
Unfocused threats. Escape along a deep, curved
river in a keeless craft that carved
smoothly through vast waves. Its sails were furled,
and it carried an unidentified cadaver
which I was trying, most clandestinely,
to deliver. And now, stark awake,
I am sitting up in bed and trying to make
some personal sense of this disturbing story,
of which I am, I know, the unwilling author.

✦ 25 ✦

I know the Rock. I spent a year and more
guarding its shores against the Soviet hordes,
who never came. A year of heat and boredom,
of swimming, chess and booze; a year of gore
and sand; of *sol y ombre*, of matadors
and miuras, swords and silks and banderillas,
across the bay in dusty Algerçiras;
of British servicemen and Spanish whores.
(I was accosted by a twelve-year-old,
and then her younger brother, by the cinema,
where I was waiting for my date, Anona,
a teacher at the R.C. Sunday School).
And, halcyon though those days undoubtedly
were, I would not live them again, not me.

✦ 26 ✦

I know Gibraltar. Three unarmed terrorists
were shot down on the very road I walked
when I was Jolly Jack Tar. And there were witnesses.
And now, today, the European court
has ruled these killings to have been 'unnecessary'.
Government's raging. Death in the afternoon
on the streets of a British territory
not of tormented bulls, but errant humans.
There's been death on the streets in Ireland too.
An English soldier shot and killed a teenage
joyrider. The army welcomed him back, though,
when he came out of gaol. (They cashier gays.)
'Well, would you want a homo in the next bunk?'
I'd prefer one to a murderer, to be frank.

◆ 27 ◆

The Gibraltar verdict has subverted the sanity
of the columnists. The UK's been slapped on the wrist
and must pay costs to the families. Of terrorists!
Yes. We who rule the waves (and rocks). Can we
be made to obey the law? Can such things be?
'Tell them to go to Hell!' one journalist
shrieks from his perch in the *Daily Mail*; 'resist
this court we must, or lose our sovereignty!'
We'll protest and pay up. The corpses will stay dead.
After some ritual posturing the hysterical
commentators will find some other matter
for rant, some other way to set their fickle
readers' adrenaline pumping faster.
Memory's short; life cheap. We're easily fed.

◆ 28 ◆

We are herded along, week after week,
by those who produce outrage to order, blaming
foreigners one week, and the next, claimants,
for all the troubles that these years of weak
government have brought; scapegoating teachers
or social workers for problems that are fundamental.
It's not mere feebleness of government, it's a general
greed and arrogance, a disease that reaches
into all parts of society, breeding a brute
insolence, sanctioned by the slick antics
of a trio of malign Michaels – the cow's lick,
the mangy lion's mane, and the grey suit
who bends the law this way and that to appease
a vicious pack of voting Valkyries.

◆ 29 ◆

It is that hour of the dusk when the room appears
ghostly in the garden, floating beyond the plate-glass
window – a fat settee, a couple of armchairs,
a side table, rest on the colourless grass;
the wall, the door, pictures and unlit lamps
slowly become firmer as the sky darkens.
We are out there too, two quiet phantasms
who sit, companionable, in the chilly garden.
It is darker now. The lawn has disappeared.
The garden is carpeted. The trees crowd closer
round the sedentary haunters of these twin rooms,
who converse with transparent gestures. And nearer
the window, the reflected furniture
stands on cement paving, lit by a trio of moons.

◆ 30 ◆

The year is moving on. It's not imperceptible
if you watch for it. Every line of trees
has its maverick. By minute degrees
the green is being subverted by subtle
faint yellows and rusty browns, the odd scribble
of tangerine is beginning to show; every breeze
collects a few more hostages; and these
day-to-day changes are quite visible
if you stay alert. But if you glance away
it all happens without you. I can remember
years when the seasons simply rolled by,
undercranked, a film speeded up: spring flowers,
roses, chrysanthemums. And suddenly December –
stripped trees, frosty breath, dark hours.

♦ 31 ♦

There's no doubt now that the trees are changing colour.
In a schoolyard in North Wales, two small birches
tint the wet asphalt with a ghost of yellow.
This is no autumn of flaming torches,
but a muted season, accepting winter's small death
without protest. The sky's a humdrum grey.
There's intermittent rain, scarcely a breath
of wind. Energy is low on such a day.
I am chauffeured everywhere and I don't make
it to the paper shop, and starved of news,
I am estranged from a world whose blood is thin
as meths, a world with little sap or juice.
The sea at Rhyl is like a placid lake.
Even at Splash Point the water ripples in.

♦ 32 ♦

In Rhyl I write this, reeling. It has been
a busy day, a day of too many children
crammed into too few, too small classrooms,
without space to move their elbows. It's obscene.
You shoehorn children into a school that is housed
in 'mobile' rooms, then consider those league tables
of accomplishment. How, from statistics, are you able
to make fair comparison? They have loused
up the system, this government, with the gibberish
of their parameters, curricula, their documentation,
and their attainment tests, their bully Ofsted
inspectors, who blunder in where they might fear to tread.
Meanwhile, packed in as close as netted fish,
the children breathe, and take their education.

Who is our guest today, children? Today …
today we have a real live poet here.
Now who can name a poet? Edward Lear!
That's very good. Yes. Michael Rosen. Gay?
That's not quite right, Louise. It's Thomas *Gray*
you mean. One more? John Keats. Excellent, dear.
And who's *our* favourite? Yes. That's right. Shakespeare –
the Greatest Poet. Who can name a play
by Shakespeare? Gwen? *Macbeth.* That's very good.
Christopher? *As You Like It.* And we do.
We love it, don't we, Christopher? Don't show it
now, Susan. Show us later, please. It's rude
to interrupt. Hands down. Perhaps our poet
will read your poem tomorrow. Sit … down … Sue.

For five days now I've been a real live poet
in two Welsh schools. We read some poems through,
we talk awhile; and then the kids get to it,
wrestling with metaphor, inventing new
space beasts, and gods, who rise up from the page
fresh-born, as real and live as any 'guest'.
Great power's released when girls and boys uncage
the imagination: an astounding zest.
And there's a willingness to try things out –
kenning, alliteration, what you will.
Fearless at best, they write unwracked by doubt,
go to the heart, unfazed by lack of skill.
And in their work they show a true concern
that life should thrive on earth, the world turn.

◆ 35 ◆

The human spirit rises above conditions;
from the cramped schoolroom comes the burgeoning song.
The parable of the sower may be wrong.
On the most barren ground the seed may ripen
into life; and I have seen advantaged children
in comfortable classrooms staring long
and glumly at their notebooks, impotent in the strong
grip of social conformity and inhibition.
It's a funny old world as the philosopher said.
A coach is racing me away from Chester;
I try to shake these thoughts out of my head,
read the paper, admire the speeding view; rest a
little; outside Oldham I gradually lose the thread,
drift … wake suddenly from a dream of disaster.

◆ 36 ◆

A hypocrite fly wrings its hands on this sheet,
hurries on minimal legs, then stops beside
the word 'disaster', gives a solemn repeat
of the concerned gesture, pauses and glides
into the air again. It is a visitation.
I share the page with another living being,
a perfectly engineered flying machine, precision
made, delicate in all its parts, which seeing
this bland white plain, scrawled over with fluent
pen marks, atlas of black tracks, investigates,
flies off, returns, runs on the page, pursuant
to a purpose and a will beyond the state
of my trammelled imagination to comprehend.
Thus, anthropocentric, I claim it wrings its hands.

♦ 37 ♦

The trees that were cut down on Primrose Hill
in nineteen thirty-eight made way for gun
emplacements. Adolf Hitler was yelling on
the wireless. Europe was shivering in the chill
wind of Nazism. The trees were lopped; the shrill
siren soon sounded. I lived nearby. One
night when I was ten I watched a German
plane, a small black cross, twisting in the pencil
probes above that hill, transfixed in the crossed beams
of questing searchlights; a terrible memory.
That was war. Here in Chekhovian Bradford it seems
our trees too must be sacrificed to technology.
To make a Town Hall car park, there are teams
preparing to cut down the cherry trees.

♦ 38 ♦

The Square looks like a military zone,
with tough wire fences and machinery –
and rubble. There's a whiff, if not of chicanery,
of clever haste. The scheme was all unknown
to us until the vote was passed. So, on
rolls progress, which seems to mean that we,
outgeneraled by the planning committee
(who meet in private), are on our own.
We can whinge as much as we like, to no
avail. The work has started and no green
activist is going to halt it. Another blow.
More ugliness. Car parks don't beautify a scene.
It's not exactly Bosnia, I know,
but aftercomers cannot guess the beauty been.

It's not a smile, it's embouchure. The brows
raised in a permanent Norman arch,
deny the speed of thought and fingers; the touch
of breath on reed is a gathering of powers.
He lifts his head, then sways the stick and blows
ripples of melody that make the heart lurch.
He reinvents a New Orleans march
parcelling it in European curlicues.
The drummer's foot stamps; the whole platform rocks.
Blow it, man, while the skinny fellow
pounds with sausage fingers the tall piano.
Give me your music. Blow that clarinet:
just one more chorus before it must be set,
broken to pieces, in its dark velvet box.

◆ 40 ◆

There is a window between us, reinforced glass.
They want to keep us apart. You sit beside
a small computer, wearing a striped blouse,
regulation. You may well be in a fright
about the new killer pill, thousands
of women are, but you treat me courteously
and are concerned that I should understand
all the restrictions which apply if I buy
a super-saver return. Behind me there is a queue
and you are new to the job. It's a busy station
and I'm worried about missing my train. 'I'd
prefer to pay by credit card.' You slide
my plastic through the machine with a crisp action.
You have slim wrists. You give me your pen to use.

◆ 41 ◆

Earlier remarks about vicars on trains
being rowdier than football fans may be disregarded.
Sunderland supporters off to the Smoke, thwarted
after a draw with Huddersfield, entertain
their fellow travellers. Tanked up they yell out
various rhythmic chants and songs and (why?)
'No surrender to the IRA.'
Sectarians know no boundaries. They shout;
it's small on melody and big on noise,
but there's no threat. They're out for the crack –
a weekend in London, a group of men and boys
without their women for a while. At Kings Cross
they surge off and form a phalanx in the concourse;
but they harm no one. Singing. Swinging their six-packs.

◆ 42 ◆

We've changed the clocks and the evenings are starker.
Leaves litter the paths, and there are berries
everywhere to be seen in the gardens, copses and hedges,
blue, shiny orange, the rosehip's scarlet, and darker,
duller reds of haws on the thorn trees. This October,
unnaturally warm and kind, has tempted
spring flowers to push through; it's all very
disconcerting and exhilarating: odd preparation for winter.
Are Oberon and Titania quarrelling again?
Or is this curious season the effect
of trapped carbon dioxide? Autumn with snowdrops!
It's weird. The birds ignore the berries; insects
are still abundant for their feasting. No rain.
But the first big winds are rattling the letter box.

◆ 43 ◆

The old anthologies are in the chest;
so I must move the radio from on top,
the coffee cup, the letters, the cassettes,
and stick them somewhere (like an old junk shop,
the living room, in seconds), then lift the lid
to face that inner chaos, kept out of sight –
I don't throw it away, I wish I did –
brown photos, programmes, school reports; they fight
for attention, like ghouls in some pernicious dream,
or like the subconscious mind made tangible,
innumerable guilts and sorrows. And, never seen
before, this seismic shift has put on view
job applications of my mother's, long ago,
signed, 'Yours Obediently, Eileen Doyle.'

◆ 44 ◆

Three years before my birth, I learn today,
she wrote, in words of schooled obsequiousness,
offering her services as governess,
a qualified teacher, with Maths and French, can play
piano and guitar. She begged to apply,
this jazz-age flibbertigibbet, whose dress
the photos show barely fringing her knees,
for posts in country houses, Obediently
signing her name. What Jane Eyre fantasies
were sidling through her mind, I wonder, when
in her elegant hand she penned this trash?
She was actress enough to have survived in those posh
mansions, sitting below the salt, her blue eyes
sardonic, her demeanour subservient.

◆ 45 ◆

I'm startled out of a dream: the alarm's a rattling
dice pot in a maze of ill-lit rooms; this shift
of the mind shakes me. I prefer to drift
slowly toward consciousness, but there's no settling
back today to meditate on wakefulness.
I know myself; I'd sleep. Feet on the floor
I start the search for clothes. Wash. Pour
hot coffee. It's dark outside. But it's time to dress,
choose a book (*Ada*) for the train today,
decide, after all, to wear a tie. It's cold.
And now in the eastern sky there's a bold
line of red. The taxi honks. I'm on my way.
A sad day trip. London. To attend
a funeral; say goodbye to an old friend.

◆ 46 ◆

One porter on the platform: his breath flies
up like cigarette smoke. The long intercity
train waits. It's not yet seven o'clock. I
board. We move off. Shipley, 7.10, the sky
on one side knicker-pink, shows a precise
edge against black roofs, with chimneys,
and aerials, a chipboard cutout for a modern nativity,
back-lit: on the other, tired blue, dark trees.
A procession of tiny Eiffel Towers, pylons,
display elegant latticing in the mist,
carefully carry their slung parabolas
across October fields; and between them a kestrel
such as Hopkins saw, no symbol of Christ,
a hungry hunter, hangs motionless.

◆ 47 ◆

The mourners are gathering outside the chapel.
It's gentle weather. Sunlight warms the grey stone
and, shouldering through the foliage, dapples
the path with shifting shadows. I stand alone,
silent for some moments, hesitant, uncertain.
His relatives are here, and old school friends.
And poets. Poets. It's like a bardic convention.
Rhymers and non-rhymers, in little knots they stand,
gregarious, darkly dressed, muted, waiting.
The chapel is crowded out. There's an address,
hymns mournfully sung, and a too brief reading
from some of the dead man's poetry – not without tears.
The coffin vanishes. And that is that.
He was a kind and witty man. He liked cats.

◆ 48 ◆

On Highbury Fields damp moulting plane trees loom,
silent and grim under a tarnished sky;
a shabby salesman in an old school tie
scurries toward a chilly furnished room.
A giggling schoolboy by the Horse and Groom
sits in a go-cart togged up like a guy;
his brothers pester hurrying passers-by
for pennies in the rainy evening's gloom.
A woman burdened with chrysanthemums
laughs with her lover, face tilts to his grin;
the steamed-up windows of the takeaway
daub yellow on the pavement's slimy grey.
A muttering tramp rifles a garbage bin;
and grimy pigeons squabble over crumbs.

✦ 49 ✦

Incessant detonations in the street
and the stench of gunpowder. Penny for the guy.
Masked effigies, too human, slump awry
like drunks by the walls, heads lolling, feet
stuck out, inert. Emotionless they await
oblivion, primed for their own neck-tie
party, with lighter fuel, matches, dry
kindling and stacked wood. On V-J night
in Beddgelert I watched a life-size dummy
of Hirohito fall into the flames
while people cheered. I thought my nausea odd,
unpatriotic, a matter for shame.
It was like this, too, when my mother died;
the sky was filled with falling flowers of beauty.

✦ 50 ✦

Red, green and gold, a pyrotechnic shower;
Martian invasion; a huge umbrella
of coloured stars hung in the smoky air
for a few seconds; a magnificent interstellar
display, beyond the window; and in the bed
the cancer did its work, the morphine, too.
Like a guy, my mother propped by pillows. I read
to her all night. 'Don't stop. I'm sure you
skipped a bit. Read it all.' Then anecdotes:
an uncle still at school, a punishment.
'Write this down.' And then, she said, the ghost
of my dead stepfather came and went.
Startled she spoke to him; silently cried,
then settled back. I read. She slept. And died.

◆ 51 ◆

She died in her own bed, the one in which
I was not born, nor anyone, a later
purchase, immense with a white headboard, rich
in eccentric detail, gloss-white moulded putti,
a scalloped frame, a theatrical bed.
While rockets pulled the crowds on Primrose Hill,
playing for a mass response, concerted
gasps and moans, she, starring among the pillows,
gave her last drama to a smaller audience:
sons, daughter-in-law, agency nurse. Grande dame
to the end, her cheek lit by the clinical transparence
of the gleaming plastic sac that fed her arm,
she played her last few lines, then paused. A door
closed. The curtain fell, and there was no encore.

◆ 52 ◆

The boarding houses on the front at Cricieth
have Vacancies. The sea slops in. There's no one
on the beach. Stones. Brown sand. We lean
on the rail. It isn't the town that's depressed
my companion. He loves his wife and children
and can't stand his job, a theme not too uncommon.
Attainment targets, endless meetings; his woman
boss bullies him. One more small death
of the spirit. He's a Careers Adviser
but seems to seek my amateur advice.
Should he chuck it all in? Live by his poetry?
(He's had some poems in the *TLS*
and two books. His wife is employed.) Or should wiser
counsels prevail? I advocate freedom, cheerfully.

◆ 53 ◆

The sea slops in. There's no one on the beach.
A cormorant hangs out its wings to dry.
Gulls drift and settle on the groin. I watch
a squat ship nose along, far out. The sky
is overcast. And there are Vacancies.
Signs hang in windows and the shops are bare.
Cafés are closed; the Welshcakes and cream teas
are gone. Eyes meet yours with a vacant stare.
We lean against the rail, backs to the town,
and gaze at the horizon. 'Yes. I booked
this week six months ago. It gets me down.
And even when I'm here, she wants me hooked
into her system.' (Curious image.) We
vacantly chat, staring at vacancy.

◆ 54 ◆

Rehearsing to read with chamber orchestra,
I adorn my copy with a mass of cryptic lore,
squiggles, words, musical tadpoles, et cetera.
These and the doodles make an eccentric score,
but it serves. I stand beside the French horn,
all aureole and plumbing; mellow fruitfulness.
My distorted image floats upside down
in a round brass bell, elongated, weightless,
curved, a Chagall lover or poet, avoiding
the dark vortex, plugged with the player's hand.
The conductor waves his wand and music comes riding
out of the silence: violins, wood, drums; a band
in which my speaking voice is an instrument.
Reeling the dactyls out, I am content.

◆ 55 ◆

The forecast had gales blowing from the south
but a glance at the ridges shows the clouds
rolling down toward Windermere. They muffed it by about
180 degrees. Their map had volleyed crowds
of busy arrows menacing Scotland;
they covered the whole of England. But the wind
has other ideas. Here in the valley bottom
it's chill; and on the Langdales there's a rind
of snow. Yet there are catkins on the hazels
this November, and though there's a mulchy scattering
of leaves in the copses, it's an autumn of puzzles,
with lots of leaf still up there, and spring
flowers in the dells. And there's a TV princess, who airs
her grievances, her illnesses, her love affairs.

◆ 56 ◆

Between the pen and the page a field of force
inhibits action. The hand moves but the ink
demurs, will not form letters, like the horse
that's taken to the trough but will not drink.
It's palpable, electric, like a wall,
impassable, of air; although I can
draw little leaping figurines, or scrawl
complex freehand mazes. The pen
will mime but will not speak. Expression stays
just beyond reach. Distress should play no part
but I've no stomach for the news these days;
for ten young girls and women were abused,
tortured and killed, dismembered, foully used.
To speak of this how do you even start?

◆ 57 ◆

You write some words. You write, 'a terrace house'.
Or perhaps you write the name of a city, 'Gloucester'.
The imagination freezes. It's no use.
You set this failure down. Or, scribbling faster,
to drown the cries for help, you write a name.
'Heather' perhaps or 'Alison'. You try
(only your hand shakes) to expunge the shame
you feel, as if this were pornography
you were writing: although you know you know
that what you are doing is trying to expiate
an evil not your own. Horror breaks through.
You write through tears. But why? It's far too late
to affect the events. The buried skeletons,
tongueless as Philomel, whisper on and on.

◆ 58 ◆

Juanita, Lucy, Carol Ann, Charmaine,
Shirley and Shirley Ann, Heather, Therese,
Linda, Alison Jane. Simply your names.
I speak them, write them down. I stare at these,
your simple listed names: Alison Jane,
Therese, Juanita, Shirley, Shirley Ann,
Linda and Heather, Carol Ann, Charmaine,
Lucy. I name you, over and again.
I make a kind of litany, to no
purpose at all. I don't seek understanding
of these barbarous deeds, but some release
from my impotent compassion, dumb anger.
Screams in the darkness. Where were the police,
Shirley? Where was God? What did He know?

◆ 59 ◆

What did He know? What did She know? Or It?
Or They? You create a universe but you
leave its maintenance to others. And so
I'll ask, 'What do I know?' and ask, 'What did
anybody know?' The women died in abject
misery in a house in a street in a city;
with lodgers and neighbours. How easily
a holocaust can happen; Jews are attacked
on Kristallnacht, while ordinary people
stand and watch; girls are prostituted while neighbours
cluck and gossip; racialist spite is disguised
in the fixed grinning iron mask of humour.
The lust for more of what we want (Now!) rises
like a virulent sickness, and resistance is feeble.

◆ 60 ◆

The world spins on its axis, a crazy roundabout,
it whizzes its riders round and round the sun.
Are we enjoying ourselves? Are we having fun?
We are. We whoop and holler and shout
as we whirl on, losing a forest here and there,
and the occasional species. We've punched a hole
in our envelope. But it doesn't matter. And on we roll,
because Now is what is important: the fun of the fair.
Sometimes we kill each other off. It's a shame
but it can't be helped; there are schedules to be met.
The goodness of the Earth is ours; and a little violence
in the taking of it can be justified. A habitat
wiped out in the process will surely come again.
What do you want? Boredom? Poverty? Silence?

◆ 61 ◆

Circles of silence shimmer like rings
on a still water, where a yellow leaf
fallen from a willow lies floating,
having disturbed the meniscus only briefly,
curled, barely touching the taut surface;
but distant from it, concentric ripples travel
like random thoughts in a circle of silence
shimmering, till they meet the edge and, repelled
by the bank, journey back toward the willow
with many complicated meetings on a water
you'd describe as still. And when another yellow
leaf settles on the pond the sequence is started
again. But sometimes in a circle of silence
all is still; time goes into abeyance.

◆ 62 ◆

No sign of sky today. One mass of murk
plasters the heavens. Starlings by the hundred
invade the garden after a shower. It's dark
even at noon. It may be that the threatened
drought is held at bay but there's no real rain.
Tankers bring water in from the North-East
(in exchange for coal?). Quiet flows the Tyne.
The Aire is famed for its pollution. At least
we excel somewhere. Schools contemplate alternate
days with no water, the taps dry, the pupils thirsty
(think of a hundred infants and no toilets).
Households are leafleted about dysentery.
Yorkshire Water dividends improve, while we are harassed.
Are the shareholders even faintly embarrassed?

December's arrived and still it looks like autumn.
I'm in the South for a reading. A spaniel
pats at my shoe and gazes up, imploring.
No walk just now. There's mist; and the annual
descent of leaves is not complete. There's that
mixture of ochreish colours up there – and
on the grass. I can see a hunched cat
stalking a starling. Every draught of wind
pulls down a few more leaves; there's a perpetual
floating procession. But there are plenty more
where they came from, though there's space to see squirrels.
Acrobatic among branches, they somersault, then soar
from one tree to the next. Winter's on hold, but
we wear our gloves, hats, scarves; button our coats.

◆ 64 ◆

Quite suddenly there's snow. The first week
of December. Sharp east winds bring massing
clouds which hump and threaten by the dark
horizon, then dump. Before a few minutes' passing
Bradford's an iced cake in a whirl of confetti.
The obstinate garden, which strung out
its death throes, leaf by leaf, petal
by petal, is docile as a Christmas card
under its covering of white. But nothing lasts;
rain has dissolved the snowscape. As fast
as it arrived it has been taken away.
Such speed! I hardly believe I've seen it:
a Winter Wonderland, a thaw (curious day),
now snow again, during the making of a sonnet.

◆ 65 ◆

On a line in a front garden in Naples Street
a teddy hangs by the neck. Literally hangs,
suspended on a length of cord, a sickly sight.
Its head lolls and its thick arms flop. It's been strung
there for days now, twisting in the wind,
slowly revolving till the string rebels,
and it unwinds, clockwise then widdershins;
like shot crows I've seen on an estate, or else
like the thousands of men and women who have swung
dangling from boughs and gantries. Hung to dry,
it has been the uncomplaining victim of freezing
fog and rain and snow. Under a dead sky
today, it hangs quite still; beneath its arm
tucked by a waggish dustman, a bin bag gleams.

◆ 66 ◆

The map is changing. Streets are cordoned off,
buildings destroyed. You see their naked innards,
scars left by stairways, gaping sightless windows,
rubble and dust. I wake in darkness. Lost
in the intricate convolutions of
a maze. I'm rifling through a junk stall, fingers
sifting the oddments, old encyclopaedias,
gadgets of unknown use. Hearing a cough
I turn, to find I'm being watched. A person
in hat and big square-shouldered coat has turned
away but I'm aware that till that moment
I'd been the purpose of their gaze, which burned
into my skin; whether it was a man or a woman
I cannot tell. Awake I'm still concerned.

◆ 67 ◆

The back door faces north. The pail I left
in the rain has forged a hoop of dirty ice,
dry and hard as iron. The air's a vice
that clamps the ribs and almost stops the breath.
I'm planting garlic. Soil, forked over only
yesterday, is rigid now; the spade strikes
and sings aloud, as though I had hit stone.
With cold red fingers I tamp in the moonlike
cloves, carefully set them in fresh compost
from my heap, which, even in this freezing
season, is warm and sweet. I chop with my trowel
at lumps, trying to form a tilth; kneeling
in white rime I imagine summer's tossed
lettuce, endives, capers – vinegar, olive oil.

◆ 68 ◆

The big beeches spread their diminishing systems
upward, black nets which trawl the darkening air,
or vein and artery charts sketched on the western
skyline, or templates for brains; they loom there
powerful with unintended meaning, this winter nightfall:
bough, branch and twig. How do I now
even imagine high summer, delightful
in succulent green, or autumn's umber show?
Bough and branch and twig: they're blacker than
the dusty city sky: and high up, hunched
like a pack of knives, a crow silhouette. It's afternoon,
just four o'clock. A fog is forming. Fists bunched
into deep overcoat pockets. I watch my breath
winding into the fog, inches from my mouth.

◆ 69 ◆

Snow, tracked by the skinny arrows of birds,
disguises everything, the walls, the walks.
The little oblong fishpond's frozen hard;
gingerly I bob the ice with my toe; it ducks,
and water seeps over its edge dissolving
the covering of snow, while someone in the house
is playing tapes of dance music; I see her revolving,
alone it seems, beyond the reflecting glass
of the french window. Slowly I release
the tilted pane of ice, which now resumes,
snugly filling its stone matrix, its place
above the black water. In one of the rooms
there is Verdi playing; the two musics share
without dispute the garden's frosty air.

◆ 70 ◆

A long flat wooden shovel in my hands
(like a For Sale sign uprooted and turned over),
I push aside the heavy snow to uncover
the hidden pathway. These are not large grounds,
just forty yards from door to gate, but it sends
the blood pumping hard, this chilly endeavour,
shifting the insistent cold invader, which never
lets up in its sly campaign, occupying as it lands,
concealing all traces. The gardens look curiously
peaceful, content under the stifling,
anaesthetic snow, which soothes, most patiently,
all fractures. And while my neighbour is levelling
his pathway I see his dark cap gradually
whitening. 'Lots more up there,' he says, still shovelling.

◆ 71 ◆

It's February now. The lake reflects
a pewter grey. In mating pairs the geese
swim line abreast, chanting their strange duets.
Neck by extended neck, they paddle. Trees
lean, still leafless, on the island. A thin breeze
hassles the meadow grass. I saunter down
to the wooden jetty, whereupon the geese
in consternation, fifty of them, churn
the surface, shouting as they go, and rise
almost as one to sail over the grey
waters, then lift and are lost behind trees
half a mile westward. Beautiful to see
these birds, broad winged and powerful; not skeined,
a travelling flock, which seeks asylum beyond the island.

◆ 72 ◆

Egyptian children are reading English poetry
in a vast school hall in Heliopolis;
or, rather, they are speaking poems from memory –
Auden and Wilfred Owen and Ted Hughes.
I have escaped a cold, extended winter
to hear them. Palms grow in gardens, the sun
splashes down on houses, domes and minarets,
the Nile flows through the city; and the children
fluently recite in the alien rhythms
of Blake and Keats. They mouth the words with love.
And at Saqqara by the pyramid,
thousands of painted ladies, inches above
the sand, escort their flickering shadows northward
to start their long migrating flight to England.

The murals at the Trianon Café
have made it to the guidebook. Art Nouveau,
erotic, oriental and *outré*,
they gloss the pages with a sensual glow.
But, in the Trianon itself, no sign
of them remains. Polished, small and square,
under dim pendulous lamps, the tables shine;
the floor is marble; but the walls are bare.
Where now are those sweet, sinuous dancing girls,
those louche pashas, that vanished opulence;
the leering eyes that eye the skirt that swirls,
the luscious drapes, the hareem decadence?
Has someone hidden that exotic glory under
a veil of matt cream paint? We sip, and wonder.

◆ 74 ◆

Durrell sat here, and Cavafy; outside
there's McDonald's burger bar, the tram station,
also the spot where Cleopatra died:
and Antony. I show the illustration,
and ask in modified English, 'Paintings? Here?'
Wordless, the waiter takes me by the hand
and leads me via the kitchens, through a door,
down a dark passage. What has he in mind?
First a partition, then an ill-lit room
with piles of linen, stacks of cardboard boxes
where men fold paper napkins in the gloom.
But on the wall, those lithe magnificent doxies
still dance, still writhe, watched by that turbaned Turk.
The folders scarcely glance up from their work.

'The first day of spring,' says Maureen at Typetec,
shrugs and casts up her eyes; and then she grins.
A glance through the window confirms it. Spring begins
this year with mist and fog, a diptych
of cold grey streets and damp housetops.
'Twenty-first of March,' she says … 'for my sins.'
I wonder about this. I'm buying pens.
'What sins, Maureen? … and I need a large notebook.'
She says that chance would be a fine thing.
And it would, this raw Novemberish day. Fine.
And sunlight would be a fine thing. And so
would pleasure. Fine. I take my pens and go,
not thinking about Maureen's sins, but mine,
and the leafless equinoctial trees, and spring.

◆ 76 ◆

Madame de Pourreu takes café au lait
in the afternoon with all the curtains drawn;
she slowly winds an elderly gramophone
and smiles: 'It was not always so, tu sais?'
A lipstick smile, très gamine, 'As you see,
there was a time …' she indictes a torn
newspaper cutting … 'one was less alone.'
The photo shows a yellowed bride. *Paris
ma ville*, repeats the thick old disc, the voice
young but obscure (the passions of a dead
crooner); a stuffed spaniel in a dusty case
stares glassily into the room. 'I said
it was not, but peut-être, it ever was' …
The room is silent as the music ends.

◆ 77 ◆ *(After Rimbaud's 'Au Cabaret-Vert')*

A week or more I'd tramped the roads and rasped
my boots on stones and flints. I came to The Old
Green Man at Charleroy, and stopped and asked
for buttered bread, and ham, which was half-cold.
Blissful I stretched my legs under the green
table; sat, gazing at the prettified
wallpaper. What a joy when sweet sixteen,
a lass with massive boobs, all flashing-eyed
(that one, she's not a girl a kiss would scare!)
laughing, brought bread and butter to my chair,
and warmish ham, on a hand-painted platter,
ham, pink and white, flavoured with just a trim
of garlic; filled my ale glass to the brim
and set it for the sun's last rays to flatter.

◆ 78 ◆

Bare to the waist I lie, and curtained off,
waiting for Debra to attend to me
(I've read her name badge). I eavesdrop. Uneasily
I hear the chat of the computer buff
who's bug-hunting beyond the drape; he laughs:
'How the hell can they expect? … look at the way
they've logged these lists … no, really my old granny
could teach them a thing or three.' Now a cough
from a fellow patient. It's 'just routine'
but I am lonely lying here and wondering
if it's *my* diagnosis that is lost in cyberspace.
Debra arrives and daubs my chest with grease,
attaches cups and flicks a switch: a juddering
from the printer. 'That's all. Tell doctor you've been seen.'

But doctor knows. The print-out's in his hand.
He has been studying my ECG,
deciphering its spiked calligraphy.
He looks me in the eye, once he has scanned
it over again, for he can understand
my angular postmodern poetry
straight from the heart; a specialist critic, he.
Those sharp irregular lines he does not find
much merit in. He says he'd have preferred
a smoother, flowing rhythm, something more
iambic; like I used to write before.
We're none too pleased. He teaches me a new word,
angiogram. The good news is, I might be in rude
health for years. The bad news isn't quite as good.

The towerblocks enclose a small green space;
groomed lawn, trees, aromatic herbs, waste bin
and windows; floor on floor of brick and glass,
everything in control, correct and clean.
Beyond the polished windows rows of desks
and wordprocessors, floppy disks and girls
(each one quite real behind her painted mask)
and men in suits, and coffee cups, and files.
Stand in the courtyard though. Look up. The sky
is blue and clear; and in that tiny scrap
the walls allow, a kestrel hovers, high
over your head, quite still, then banks and swoops
gliding serenely in tight looping curves,
a fearsome alien in this ordered world.

♦ 81 ♦

The tent is floored with lumpy okra matting,
and brightly lit by small electric floods;
a heavy-breasted nude sprawls on her bedding
(she's framed in gold); cats, landscapes, pagan gods,
in simpler frames compete – there are vases, too,
masses of flowers, lilies in abundance –
and various oddities, a nun, a shoe.
The sundial looks peculiarly redundant.
Outside the sun is shining. It's Easter Sunday
and there's a clash of bells – a village wedding.
Here there's painting, sculpture, lace and that clever
jewellery. But it's the awkward floodlit sundial waiting
for all this canvas to be taken away
that calls to the eye, among this high endeavour.

♦ 82 ♦

A plump crow in a blossoming cherry tree
stumbles and hops from twig to branch, bobbing
the boughs. Clumsy. Lout in a lingerie
department. Insolent border guard, grubbing
through intimate belongings, thick thumbs
and gloved fingers shifting papers and clothing
and toilet preparations. So May comes
with a cold wind and ragged clouds scooting
over a pale sky, with washing blown out straight,
shirtsleeves reaching for the horizon. The crow
lumps his way through, hustling his weight
and bulk, scuffing the bright petalled snow –
a dozen brushstrokes of shiny black paint –
opens his dark bill, gives voice, a harsh complaint.

◆ 83 ◆

A century and more has passed, and still
the Duddon glides over its stony bed.
Upstream thin clouds tumble across the hill,
a drinking heifer lifts her questioning head.
Near one wide boulder, a small turbulence,
where water humps then fans to scatter spray,
sharpens the river's music. There's a sense
of time entire, told in a single day –
of seasons gone, of afternoons that pass
in squandered minutes, unregarded hours.
Where buttercups stipple the unsheared grass,
ferns spread green hands by rusting clover flowers;
the Duddon moves, its waters clear as glass,
through fields where leaning foxgloves shake their towers.

◆ 84 ◆

The sun is shining and the great man's gone.
The lunch crowd takes its coffee on the terrace.
Three girls run giggling across the lawn
to Tennyson's sundial. Its motto, *Horas
non numero nisi se* ... incomplete,
the plinth engraved with family names, the lines
from *In Memoriam*, they ignore. Their feet
tap at this emblem of the power of time,
that's halted like a stopped clock (for the gnomon
is gone; the numberless dial's untouched by shadow).
The poet's presence still, although invisible,
broods over this parched lawn, these idling girls,
the watching guests who sit by the tall french window,
whose time is now ... will perish ... and so on.

Sudden and violent, the warm June rain
storms down. It beats at flowerbeds and spatters
mud onto garden paths. It floods all gutters,
sends swollen rivers eddying round drains.
It strips the petals from the peonies;
they lie in heaps under the flattened bush.
We close the windows and watch swagged runnels slush
down the panes. For ten minutes it pours; pennies
from heaven, not. As suddenly, it is still.
Steam rises from the path. The peony stamens
show white and naked, and there's the smell
of washed summer air. We look for a rainbow
but find instead, pared fingernail above the chimneys,
the newest of moons, transparent in the fading blue.

A NOTE ON THE POET

Gerard Benson was born in London and now lives in Bradford. In a long and varied career, he has been a sailor, a clerk, a waiter, an actor (touring the North with Century Theatre), a teacher, and a lecturer with over twenty years at the Central School of Speech and Drama. He was a leading member of the performance poetry group The Barrow Poets, and is one of the prime movers of the remarkably successful Poems on the Underground (soon to go Overground). He travels widely in Britain and abroad to give readings, and is well known for his poetry workshops with both adults and children.

As a writer for children he has achieved considerable recognition, winning the Signal Award in 1991 and being nominated for the prestigious Carnegie Medal in 1996. His appointment in 1994 as the first Poet-in-Residence for the Wordsworth Trust at Dove Cottage in Grasmere enabled him to work widely in Cumbria, especially in schools. It was during his year in Grasmere that he wrote *In Wordsworth's Chair*, a collection of poems published by Flambard in association with the Wordsworth Trust in 1995. *Bradford & Beyond* has emerged from a lifelong love affair with the sonnet form in all its varieties. Some of these 85 sonnets are Shakespearean, some Petrarchan, while many are hybrid, yet throughout this *Journal* in verse Benson is constantly inventive in revitalising the traditional fourteen-line form in a distinctly modern way.